FOREVER ALIVE

FOREVER ALIVE

Fran Lock

DARE-GALE PRESS

First published in Great Britain by Dare-Gale Press, 2022

Dare'Gale Press, 15-17 Middle Street, Brighton BN1 1AL
Correspondence: editor@daregale.com

www.daregale.com

Distributed by Central Books

ISBN: 9780993331183

Poems © Fran Lock, 2022

Thanks are due to *Militant Thistles* and *Culture Matters*, where a number of these poems first appeared.

All rights reserved. No part of this publication may be reproduced, stored in a retrieval system or transmitted, in any form or by any means, electronic, mechanical, photocopying, recording or otherwise without the prior permission of the copyright holder and the publisher.

Cover image: Edvard Munch, 'On the Waves of Love', burnished aquatint and drypoint, Art Institute Chicago.

Typeset in 10/11pt Delicato, designed by Stefan Hattenbach.

Printed in England by TJ Books on munken paper certified by the Forest Stewardship Council.

Dare-Gale Press is committed to carbon neutral and environmentally conscious publishing. For our environmental policy please visit www.daregale.com.

Contents

The last wolf killed in Ireland	7
Our War	9
The policeman knows	11
Fear of sand	13
Poem in the Year of the Wran	15
Reprise	16
The Moors	19
The Country Wife	21
Sempervivum	23
At the wake/ in the wake	25
Dissociate	27
What the world calls trauma, you called the birdhouse in your soul	30
Tragic backstory	31
Master of all you survey	34
A stuck record	36

For Marty, and for all of us

The last wolf killed in Ireland

'... for every bitch wolfe, six pounds; for every dogg wolfe, five pounds; for every cubb which prayeth for himself, forty shillings; for every suckling cubb, ten shillings; and no woolfe after the last of September until the 10th of January be accounted a young woolfe, and the commissioners of the revenue shall cause the same equallie assessed within their precincts...'
Oliver Cromwell, 7th April 1652

mac tíre, strange aggressor. my name a subtle heckle on an english tongue. to say my name invites the mountain: mountain of malice, hill of hides, the snow-quilted *sliabh* between fort and forest, stronghold and stream. the night is full of saints and toads. *fuil, feoil,* my young son a fallen aril, stepped to stain. big men, in the paranoid plainclothes proper to thieves. our pelts become pennants along their border wall. their arrows break off in my boys. *mac tíre*, aconite's *aisteach* tincture, a pale green bane most verdant after grief. big men erect a republic of bone. *osraige,* ossory, ossuary state. through the horny gloaming, their gimp tread and bilious crooning. a ruined harvest, a feudal moon. my eye is gold, and it taints whatever it touches; gilds whatever it spoils. *this* was my mountain. i had such husbands, lean and lairy, courting my carnal skulk by culvert, verge and hollow. our sex a vernal effort, *piseóc*-sweet. to hex, to bless, their breath was meat and burning sage. these, my suitors: lank flags flown from paring blades. big men, who estimate their skins by weight. *mac tíre*, indulging my jugular thoughts alone. revenge is a dish best served sprinting over

dawn's ditch. what would i give to swallow
them whole? the very towns are teething,
mouthing a murderous vowel meaning
home. this was never their home: towers
and turnstiles, roads and gates, their steely
premonitions of decay. i lope frustrated
light to dread, enter a hateful song aslant.
the shunned house and the haunted tor.
fáel. fail. the plane. the moor.

Our War

'We who had nothing will school them in serenity'
Seferis, *Mythistorema*

here, at the chattering turn of the year,
you tarry in my flashbacks. those men
who speak of *the land*, the dark knot
fouled into fastening, tight at the throat,
night after night. would tar my eyes
like sheep sores, sleep. but no. here,
in the cold, damp gape of a wellington
boot, the spitters and widows,
the weavers of orbs. those men who
sing of *the land*, fallow or sodden,
would stride it to possession. how
the mouth succumbs to psalms, to
sand, my thick tongue sculling
a coronach. the church has her
congregations, wraiths of crude
carousal, lighting little tapers.
look! and a small child rivets his
peaky stare to a flammable angel,
the angel an effigy made of itself.
bonfire boys, with pockets full
of boiling gall. young men who
talk of *the war*, its sprawling zeitgeist,
as if they knew more of the earth than
its currency of tubers. as if they'd
known fear's soft aftershow. i hear
them speak, and i am newly sickened.
here is history, pallidly lurking.
here are the birds: the sparrows
of abandon, a cursory gospel of gulls.
here are our people, yours and mine,
in the grey-pink battery flesh
of the poor. and who are we, but
a rumour in the works of the sea?

between *task* and *quest*, our ship
turned back. or sunk. sweetness, our
ancestors lived through their limbs,
through the slippery wakeful nonsense
of whatever work: biddies patching
canvas sails, menfolk lost on dredgers'
errands. the canals mouthed us home.
we knew, who cannot claim *the land*,
the sea gives up. in the mute slant, in
the stale tang of lay-by and boarding-
house. where the turf is cut. in a bothy
light. in a flinty cowshed light. in
a scaldy light. in a caravan light just
so. there are men who juggle
the glamour of crisis like swords
then apply for arts council funding.
i am tired, refine the nervous sugar
of your name, where everybody
speaks your name to football chant
or skipping rhyme to a *you're shit*
sing-along horny on shore leave.
my student says: *art can only be
redeemed by the expenditure of reason.*
i cannot imagine anything more
nauseating or less true. i dream of you.
all our boys, bursting between words,
pouring through the great white still
of the world, through the gullet
of the world, swilled in the gob
of the world between grim obeisances.
here, at the chattering turn of the year,
i return. and the tongue turns chalk
to walk your silhouette to incident.
dear, one, when they speak of *the land*
it is not this: spliffy morning, spoofed
aurora, wasted love. an elegy for many
hands. you are dragged in the wake
of a broken plough.

The policeman knows

a killing is called for. your romany man
for *a frankenstein*. tomáš, a necessary
neck. you inhabit the holes in his eyes
forever, your fine mouths boarded up,
your deaths both cheap and pure. your
bodies are packets of stale contraband;
the glorious fact of your shadow, a witch.
you are beaten with sticks until your own
mouths evict you. you cannot inhabit
even your breath. spit on your shadow.
the policeman knows what is left
of you: a barren sleeve, the candle
consumed by its thin *no comment*.
the split hairs of refusal, turning white.
he knows you will not emerge into
magic. there is only death
and its council of arrogant spades,
sifting the earth into absolutes. in
the end, you are denied even fire,
that slender escapist, best and other
self. the policeman is made of bronze,
of granite, of headline. the world
casts models from his monotone.
each night, he consecrates his
meltweight to the scales, pleased
by what he's gained. his kneeling
knows no prayer. your faces dwell
in his mythology of mirrors. he sees
you looking back at him and is afraid.
his counter-spell is gravity. do not go
shirtless and feather-weight into
the night, or throw your convulsive
survival at the world. crouch in
corners, shrink. he will wade in you
up to the waist. in the silvery
destitute streets you have no right

to walk, he will walk on you.
the policeman knows where
to redeem your teeth, if necessary.
they will open you up: appropriate,
proportionate. as it was in teplice
and anywhere. as it is, will be, world
without end. the policeman knows.
the cracked rib he calls god is on
his side. oh, to be washed. to be
washed clean. to be washed clean
away.

Fear of sand

For Rob

some faces are entitled to their violence:
touch them and they fly apart like broken
scissors. there are soldiers, and then there
are *soldiers*, he says. in his dictionaries
of tin, arranged in rows. the man on my
left was afraid of sand. the opposing poles
of his blue-grey eyes, refusing to meet in
the middle-distance. an acrid, irrigated sky.
there's a smile that comes off on the back
of your hand: scorched red rubber, these
things i know. these things you do not
understand he says: *shellacking, flack,*
the scalloped edges of a liar's tongue.
a world unmade and glittering. some
faces are formed around the question:
will there be cherries in heaven? in
a light syrup tasting mostly of styrofoam.
*will anyone care that we burnt the bibles
we swore on?* it is late, alone. the dog
disputes the manger; the body of christ
climbs back into his porcelain babies.
the body of christ, resplendent in
a shrapnel of candied fruit. the infant
jesus, a fossil in tar. it is late: in the film,
a rich widow strips gold embellishments
from her ears, and her arched neck is
checkov's gun, pre-empts the guillotine. in
the dark, a man is bringing his hammer
down on a cow's head like judge's gavel.
somewhere, a neck is being wrung, or
the cursory light of the candle is bobbing
to mass. my mind is racing. i have firework
emojis in all the strategic areas, preserving

what we'll call my *modesty*. but i am falling
apart in front of strangers. to my
doctor i say *it was like this* or *like that*.
but my own name is absurd to me,
the debris of metaphor. the man on
my left was afraid of sand, of even
the crust that he picked from his eyes.
it yellowly hardens. he turns it to glass.

Poem in the Year of the Wran

to wake, not to bury. poet and dog
have passed through the long dark
night of the distended gut. and morning
is coughwort and toadflax; virgin's
tears and sorcerer's violet. will
the hedgerows afford us a funerary
bird? nature concussed between
winter's toll and spring's gloved
quickening. there are *garlands
for the dead, and crowns for
the condemned*. there's a moist
green mouth that swells the meat
it holds. hawks we have, turning
their renunciate masks toward
the power lines. and the garlic
breath of sabotage. this we can do.
but the wran? a bird we tell
like a bead. no. grandfather, squinting
through the aspic of his cataracts
at a country sorely changed, where
speedwell wears the rumour
of its blue, where fallen leaves
are physic's echo, starlings
excavate themselves like wet flints
from a civil field. where is
the wran? that fat molecule
of promise, the genius of furze.
little obeah, monarch
of the sorrels. of stale bread
and sour milk. her government
is exile, the sceptre and the orb.

Reprise

even now there are places where a thought might shrink –
a mind worked out and thwart with waltzy boozing, hot
with speed, still wearing all its frenzy on its sleeve. to breathe
this bitter vigilance undone. abused, becalmed, the gilded
anchors slack. to melt, exult, to rid ourselves of all those
token torments. there are places, yes. we burn his letters in
the sink, hold them by the dog-ears of their disregard. he
was so young, and feckless in that state of being smitten.
even now the sky grows smashed to say the laggard
thunder of his name. you have to wonder at that suit
of clothes coarsened into a man. had *he* recourse to ball
his fists to fossil in the pockets of his loss? he mouths our
idling maps to fire. *ire-land*, word full of wasps, of paucity
and nausea. he looks over his shoulder, a convict crossing
himself in the yard. i think not. i think they do not grieve,
cannot. have never dragged themselves down streets
concentric with offence and fought another cruelly cresting
thought. there are no ghosts, striding in the violence
of their migraines keying cars. years of hopeless gluttony,
and autumn has arrived, in dejection and arrears; pyracantha,
hacking cough, with flight and threat in each averted eye.
ilex, cornus, callicalpa. we are here, touching up the hoary
edges of our need. there's a voice, drawls the collodion
strophes of his death. wooden boy, notches in his bedpost
body cut. once and always, our continuous entire. a crow
is mourning's stooge, cracked along its chorus, wakes me,
pledging feathers to the costume of my guilt. and poetry
paints its swooning mottoes *every*where. it is no good.
flowers without language, this loss: eyes puckered with drink,
more bleeding than is good for beauty, the genial and fake,
the frankly murderous. there are places. some steward
of a soft embrace enfold me. you have to wonder. not
expression, but *escape*, wearing the bronze rosettes of brazen
remedy. does he know what it means, wearing our variant rose
in the crook of an arm, on the lips against grace, to sharpen

the starving body into sleep? the clock is an enemy, rapt with
strategy. they are mostly gone, who stammered their eclipse
in council eyries, squats, and singing: sweet lagan, run
weary till the end of my song, till all our lustres numb, till daybreak's
craven conjuries, till kingdoms come and *auld folks* trade
their chitties in for loose tea, till sailors step out of their shanties,
till i meet my zealous, perishable neighbour in the street and do not
spit, till i am no longer spat *at*, till all my gammon covenants run
blood, till my own country knows me, till i am not her inmate or
her exile, till the end of time. sweet lagan, run swiftly, till our dead
in their shining lethargy are lifted up, till the television voices
number *gypsy boys* among the culled. even now, as autumn
arrives with old campaigns begun afresh, we are finding ways
to kill this thought. i'd made a book his bed, the mattress
and the mire i flipped, end over end. the ciphers of a metered
time, and laid on lambswool narrowly. i run my finger round
the rim of love. it sings its whimming posey till it shatters.
he says no, there will be no laying down. no one to break
amends like bread. *home* will not be fuchsia, nor a stream striven
clear. when i look at our maps i will see my grandfather's hands.
when i hold my grandfather's hand i will see blue lines
ploughed into boundaries, will see life's suffering, impaled
upon a hangnail. home will be any arbitrary nightmare, the whining
of a child-bride kept in a closet, will be telescopes trained on
an exit wound, garrotte, cavort, galley-bondage. gangrene, greed
of sick natures. the hairshirt and the shipwreck. the counterfeiting
light refines whatever it touches. and by *refines* a kind of scraping
off. and still i hear that voice, those voices, and i have been
eating these arsenic vowels so long my tongue turns tragedian
too. lyric has this writhing sweetness to it. flags in their fascist
semaphore. he said *a flag is mostly air, biddy,* how a halo slips,
how a mouth is mauled. and i know and i know, but i love
the grave that grew you, boys. though all her walls have ears
inclined to eavesdrop times, though august is a punitive crescendo,
though our church had blessed the blueshirts, worn the polished
turd of tyranny, and despite the dosses, kips, the own goal in
a celtic shirt whose native language is noise. despite the bark stripped

from the trees, the necromancy of nostalgia, zombie militias rising
from the nearest limepit, haunting an english dream. although she is
a b-movie. although she is the spectacle of queer bash
and revenge porn. although she is misogyny, an *enfant's*
trembling rhetoric of lust. i loved *you*, and love makes me mediocre
with longing. you have to wonder, has longing ever possessed
this creature like a terror? brain sticky with the latent prints
of an old pain, rising; missing a friend, a lover, a father, a daughter
whose voice made morning? those lost and those returned. presumed
and absolutely. a hurting fact there is no gospel for in *any* language.
when he wipes his arse on our peace he kills them again. and again.
those whose deaths run hot, and those whose mirror is the serpent's
mouth in trying to forget, has always been. there are places –
hanging in the see-through gelatine of our injuries. but Pig Thief,
miscreant and mutable, whose name a shadow valentine i trace
across my tongue like parmar violet charm against their heresy.
there is a staying with. there will be dynasties of upturned faces,
blued onto the incidental day. the young. may their griefs be held
in the palm of a hand, palmed like marbles, rolled away, all infamies,
attritions shrugged. we will care for them. like silence cares, like light
and space, and dig ourselves in with a gentle spade when time has done.

The Moors

After John Clare

and he says to me: how
will we know spring now,
without those couriers of soft
arousal? birds. our lips pinched
with nervous thirst. we breathe
a warm sleet meaning *fire.* deep
peat burns. how will we know?
when the year turns, measures
the milky length of itself in
driven grouse. the moor all
wet, sequestered death. fix
an occasion to cold, blue
smoke, to blades of grass
like blackened wicks.
seasons we have borrowed
back from flame. the river
hauls itself to haunting:
bampot lazarus, bent upon
flood, a grey lace grazing
the eyelets of windows.
meadow-mauled and gasping,
we will learn new alphabets
of ruin. the unrequited
gekkering of rusty ghosts:
a fox throwing its frail
amours at an empty night.
there is no wren, to bury
or to wake. a rake of ash.
man sized in dirty straw.
a hare is a quarrel of small
bones, stale fur, is anything
turned or scrubbed or beaten
back. her eye a bead of amber

trespass still. it is still.
lesser cinder, smothered.
to pick those thinning threads
of flesh from soil; not meat
enough to bait a hook.
and spring will mean a *chavi's*
fist, raised against the formal
hurt of crows, a hedge without
scent, a halting rumour of stoat,
of rabbit. sodden hips, rotten
haws, recipes of dog rose, sloes
and galls. *bedeguar,* as ague's
swollen auger, telia tied
and thick with misery. how
will we know? through murmur
perfect to alarm. by the wire,
of course, its counterfeit
nativity of stars. sackcloth
scope of the moor, mile
upon mile. and residues
on remnant winds. we, who
lived lightly and divided
through our exile shed
the false hope of return
in fences. measure our timid
griefs against the stench
of gutted heather.

The Country Wife

how my face is a pillow,
and your fist finds repose.
sleep, my frenzied pencil.
sleep, audacious haunt
of fox. sleep has hung her
wet deterrent in the trees,
says *come not near.* now
hunger shuts my mouth.
now hunger drums
a buzzard from the copse.
he is a cleric's jest of wing,
shadow of his former
mardy wheeling. between
the silo and the road, all
the obstinate tenants
of the hedge. where fear
will stretch the pained
decency of sparrows; blue
sky benumbs like an egotist's
mirror. nature, without
pity or apology; malice
or mercy. see, a charm
of maggots passing through
the wreck of a sheep. see
pigs, lilting eunuchs
of the sty. where bullocks
sway in their stalls
like morbid lordlings,
see. and god is here,
dragging a knife through
your idle surmise. he is
always here, folded as
small as a *scottish promise*
in the snug wallets
of our folly. sisters, those

christly automata,
pulling their teeth out
with pliers to make more
room for prayer. sisters
in a pavilion of bells,
mouthing their sinister
forbearance to the walls
but tenderly. and they
are also sheep, in the group-
think of their grazing,
who live mostly in the supple
arrears of the tongue, what
grace shall never utter.
winter: we do not decay,
we are consumed.
my fury a circular pact
with this body, your dissolute
mourning, its trail of vicious
appetites. your fists
in a crouching light illiterate.
omens of no account.
sleep, my thrown voice.
sleep, carving my sensitive
flesh into limelight,
transmuting my vow into
wound. to look upon beauty –
i shall not, it is the museum's
remedy. our boy, his body
mocks the warm fuzzies
of your elegy. husband,
whose hands have turned
to hooves in the dark;
stallion of lesser extremities.
my night mount,
concussion's confessor. say
it again: ice, this melody.
the wages of rain.

Sempervivum

it was you all along, angel of crabapple
intercourse. my failed stranger, you'd
counterfeit furies to frighten me. *me!*
poor little buttercup, and city mornings
thick with bacon and saline. dirty windows
hold a rheumy heat. nothing grows. nothing
grows except these asexual rosettes i pin
to earth by slender threads of succulence.
forever alive. an ulcer tempered, a thunder
tamed. our *inward heats:* the house,
the heart, fretting and inflamed. the radio
commits its batshit hymns to summer.
the houseleeks grow epiphanies of flesh:
an aureole, an areola, mauve and porous
place of stones. july dilates, and august crawls.
virid warheads, jellies, red eruptions slick
as veal. an apron of unwelcome light
across the yard. downy buboes, bulbous
domes. this spatulate extravagance of hands.
rubra, spreading like an enervated buddha,
tight with livid fat. *nothing grows,* you say.
nothing grows but with an eerie fury under
an antipsychotic sky. the whole world pink
and pastelled to compliance: seroxat,
peroxide, paroxetine tones. no life except
the ditty-dreams of birds. no life except
the accidents of lightning. the hawk is a dry-heat
hangs in the air, and you could strike a match
against your eye. the dog in a shit-stirred state
like a matinée zombie. your hand coming apart
in the theatre of his teeth. the rainbow sings
of antidotes and patents. take twice daily
with food. *forever alive,* the fractals
of a black nest, forensically vamped. imagine.
the green fang swelling with our sickness.

it's in us now. prostrate with fever, while
the day curls back along one ragged edge.
they're spilling from the gutter, crowding
out the eaves. you, in a fatalist garland.
nothing grows except. this horoscope,
this horror. a budding pungent fate.

At the wake/ in the wake

it wasn't very wife of me
to answer the night, its cagey
lunar imperative. i've carried
my pain like a fabergé egg
in the hollow of a spoon.
otkaznik – those who are
denied become those who
will refuse. baby, and with
bratty tenderness, sing it
with me: *i have no home.*
when you're not welcome
within even your own
razored strut, there's nothing
to do but funnel your worst
ideas down the fouled seam
of a tongue. a fulsome dirt,
a fatty sky, and coffee
like cocaine is but a tempest
in an artery. life is so near,
i could lick those lighted
windows, melt their
curtained kitchens in my
mouth.
i'm not a nice person.
consult my cells, invent
fresh sickness, measure
me up for the houndstooth
suit of simplified affection:
*they'll love you when
you're dead.* or not at all.
you know me, my eyes trap
their anthropology inside
of them. i'm digested alive
by my own stupid daring.
inside of me: dirtbags,

glandular trash-talk, not
enough sawdust to
soak up the blood.
why did i come? city,
sad den of copyrighted lust.
poets, and their swooning
freight of diseases: homeland,
family, full sexual history.
i stand in the centre
of a dark room and men
do their conversation at me.
i can see through his skull
to his brain, sealed in
a tepid vacuum, sandwich
at an automat. here now,
and briefly, nervously alive.
curse my wrists, necrotised
with silver. how it burns
when a hand brushes
mine. a sticky trace
against her skin: fish
scales, brightest cycloid,
a mucus regiment.
to be carnivorous, predatory,
extinct. drink the gentrified
dark, torrid in time-lapse.
common aconitum, *addicted
to poison*. i do not belong
to my body. to the stroppy
runes and slang we make
for meaning. one day,
their heads will be the eggshells
i walk upon. thumb through
a fontanelle, fisting wet fruit.

Dissociate

it wasn't me. except
it was: days of steadfast
purpose and patrol, just
barely glimpsing daylight
in between the blades
of secateurs and self-
control.

it wasn't me. except
it was. mockery as
compliment's caramel.
day after day,
the neighbourhood
boys throwing rocks.
down latitudes of dull
pursuit, to tease a tooth
to ruin. braces, glasses,
long white socks.

it wasn't me. but then –
the night is a hopeless
praline fissure; my own
face in the mirror: a beige
informer, sticking out
her tongue.

to sleep all day
and wake exhausted.
to sit around in
waiting rooms.
the west-indian
nurse is singing,
her heedless
aviary tongue.

it wasn't me. except.
i don't lose time,
i put it on:
one-thousand-and-one
loitering disgraces.

my null form is a vow
it breaks apart in drift-
wood, barnacles, the torn
hull of all my mithered hours.

i wasn't me. except.
and here we are,
stoking the blue furnace
of twilight. the garden
smells sweet, and you
say: *the rose, that dizzy
rhapsodist of thorns!*

yes, i remember you,
except when i don't.
and by i: the axe
disputing the tree,
the tree suppressing
the axe.

it wasn't me who
thought to be happy.
gathered my atonements
into a ring toss:
confiscated halos.

sometimes. and men
like him, rubbing
hisself against a dirty
little nuance. will we
ever be free of posh

boys? tugging at
themselves, would
paraphrase an open
fly.

how you want to say:
here i am, fuckers, i was
here all along!
i'm a boy too,
my luminous reach.

oh holy night of utmost
temerity. the champagne
tastes like bloody gravel,
i've covens in me, pouring
out of my mouth.

a breathtaking fuck,
the mannered thirst
of an english drunkard.
capital, the relentless
morgue of it, a futile
rune meaning wilderness –
anything cut in the back
of the skull.

look me in the briar
patch where my eyes
should be. how it
wasn't me. a rat in
a velvet bag.
looking out,
chewing through.

What the world calls trauma, you called the
birdhouse in your soul

as it were. ill feelings, bleakly
honeyed. a hospital dream again
last night. the conflagrant farce
of your self-destruct returns
to haunt me: die hard sequel,
wearing *with a vengeance*
on your face. finding the tiny
pearl of your pulse. yellow eye
of dolent focus pulled. i am
watching the monitor, reading
my lines from its bogus
autocue. *follow the bouncing
ball.* alive is a flaccid miracle.
inertia breeds fatigue. these
swooners after morphine,
the sluggish shades
of succour. when you speak,
you float a stagnant gospel
into air. this weak stink is
the *odour of sanctity*. dear,
my thumbprint pressed in
the wet wax of your spasm,
pushed through softened
irrepare. in the dream, i am
not afraid. i do not taste
my own lips, deadened in
apology. i court your stale
gaze hotly. seek fulfilled
infection in a kiss. i wish –
but it always ends the same:
that song, little worm, little
emissary of the ear.
an empty bed, the sheet
a linen silence i embroider
into poem.

Tragic backstory

i am gothic with apathy on afternoons like this.
hope will not be bludgeoned into luck, and all
my lovelies gone. i tool away at grief, sailorboy
working an oath into a tusk with the lampblacked
scrimshaw of injured spleen. this house is full
of ghosts: chorus of drowned captains, quacking
in the mildewed quandary of their song. mute
victorian suicides, daffy brides, bound up in
coroners' bombazine. poets, squealing their
iambics in the thumbscrews of regret. if not
the house, then myself, with ulcered thoughts
encircled, nights. sky without stars, sabled to
endangerment, a storm at sea. me, corpsy
virgin in the formal cerements of want. i ready
the worm that will undo me. in my mouth. *oh!*
by which i mean i pithed a plucky rose for
you, i lit a candle in the church. by which i
mean i sat, milking their cringy sermons for
proof. in the weak nausea of belief i traced
your heat with my desperately seeking. there
was blood on the sheet. it was mine. they
died in the winter, wiping their snouts on our
pity, lungs florid with rot. they were poets,
their pockets grew cheap tubercles of coin.
winter, with its instinct for sputum. and i
grew fat green chancres against despair. my
lean-to bloomed with vernal smut. i grew
convulsive and syndromal, secreting a bland
lyric meaning chemo, cocaine, menopause,
any rumoured thing. i have been sealed
inside the diplomatic bag of this pain for so
long now, i don't know what i'd be without
it. elsa, perhaps, in a white grave-smock.
elsa, and the leaky scaffold of her hair.
elsa, sutured and improved. elsa, hissing
in the fevered kitsch of nineteen thirty-

five. elsa. the pearly morgue of her
uterus. elsa under blacklight
fluorescing. elsa lanchester: both
mary and monster. here i am, deserted,
cured in the coppery threat-light
of plague, and i numbly crusade
through the lesser hours of viral pay-
load, longing. how easy to deliver
oneself of a chic *nachträglichkeit*,
to spit the never-ever night that
clings to talk. how easy to step
through the neck of an edith head
gown and disappear. how easy to
drown. or to kick from your clothes
at the ciphermost stretch of the sea.
this house is full of ghosts, but you
are not one of them, falling instead
through the golden fault-line of my
metaphors. *how easy*, i said, but it's
not: the body runs up against itself,
is the goddess niké, beheaded. her
bladed wings are paring the difficult
world. these ghosts belong to the sea.
now, voyager, girdled by its blue
and sighing regard, you too return
to the tightness of water. *oh!* by which
i mean your books are boats tonight.
i cannot sleep, the tv is death-penalty
apologists, the sugary toil of a popular
song, thick people crying over power
ballads, tory politicians playing their
smirking guilt on a wurlitzer. i am
a gothic folly. i gestate a tide of salt.
move through the thorny loins
of the night, its barracks of black wire
hair, the four and twenty black gulls
backed into a corner, baked inside

this moon. i will *not* be mad. i will also
rise and assume the halting brilliance
of fire. but today i will only contemplate
the bluebird at my shoulder, *the snake up
my sleeve*. i crown you cleanly among
my phantoms. with an oracle's kiss,
an intended wound.

Master of all you survey

or say *laird,* rather.
tomcats, darkly cruising,
the rent boys of animal
enterprise. i remember it
this way: the bruised
and quickening musk
of dying plants. with
nightmare abridged
into email, a brinicle
plumbing the heart.
was i making the sound
of a screwed pig? yes.
did i tear my tights?
did soft little furies
constitute themselves
like boiled bats in my
potty-mouth? did i say
a wet *fuck!* into the floor
one thousand-thousand-
thousand times? yes.
and also yes. i was
a surly termite,
burrowing into denial.
i went to work on
monday. gum under
the lip of the desk.
the meeting is *sorry,*
as fake as stale porn.
i remember it this
way: a lethal snake.
the tepid scent
of pleasure,
cauterised at source.
the pit bull's scuppered
tummy as he licks

my eyes, as he places
a stuffed dinosaur in
my lap. i remember
running, until my legs
hardened into stilts
of wax. or knives
that trapped my body-
heat in their blades.
i squirmed under
a landfill of stars,
of moons no use to
metaphor. and tomcats,
reflecting yellowly,
this shrunken world
small in their eyes.

A stuck record

i built my house of straw. i built
my castle out of sand. i built my
church in the lion's mouth. amen.

+

there is no fate sweeter than
fetters of fire. a rose completes
the cellblock wall.

+

a blackthorn stick in the burden
of its bludgeon. joys will be illicit
and then cancelled. green wood
glimpsed through a crack in
the hurley.

+

i built my house of straw,
in this desert of tempered
returns, in this city its sly
vocation of coffins. i built
my church in a miser's
purse.

+

in the night *they* broke in
and moved all the furniture,
replaced our family photos
with the catalogue faces
of strangers. our flag is
a *kick me* sign, flown at
half-mast.

+

did i say *our flag?*
i meant *my face.*

+

one day i'll catch them,
a trebuchet's boiling rebuke.
ask not for whom
the bell tolls, father-
fuckers. you protestant
oompah loompahs,
it tolls for thee, i'll say.

+

her holiness fits her, tight
as the skin of a wet apple.
there were days when *dole*
meant sorrow, *parole* was
a june bride softened with
promise. words have been
lovely, even in english.
now the tongue in its stretch
of slow rue. names collect
and recoil in turn: your
name, her name, mine.

+

she has the night,
its inherited leather,
lips pressed together
in mummified
schtum. nocturnal
creature, running

through the weekend's
reeling thrift of stars –
my child.

+

defaced the pennies
in her pocket just to
spite herself.

+

my girl, my girl,
to the gargoyle soundtrack
of a secondary modern.
when they called her
terrorist she rose up
like a wasp, resurgent.

+

i built my house of straw.
on the bones of pale confessors,
buried alive in the kerry green
golf shirts of their fathers.
i built my castle out of cards.
my church was a heart shaped
swimming pool, was a pimped
ride, was a thirty foot trailer,
was a white merc with fins.

+

just kidding. i built my church on
the moon, from the blood money
of millionaires.

+

my girl is learning the major
arcana, an expendable prodigy,
writing us over and over again
through the shivering guilty
hours before dawn.